The Dragon in the Sea

Story and Design by D.A. DeWitt
Illustrations purchased from Vectorstock.com
Copyright © 2015 D.A. DeWitt
ISBN-13: 978-0692595862
ISBN-10: 0692595864

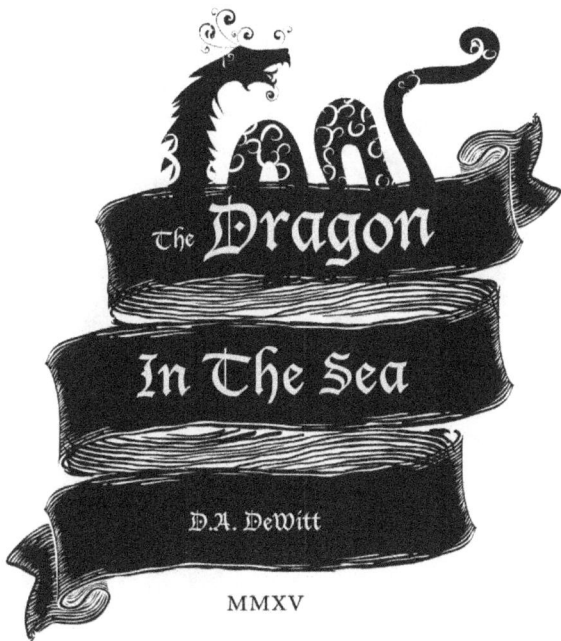

The Dragon

In The Sea

D.A. DeWitt

MMXV

THEOLATTE PRESS

To my three sons & Addi:
another dragon story of
truth & orthodoxy.

The following story was found on a parchment sealed in a clay pot buried deep inside a cave in northern Asia Minor. The parchment was torn on both ends suggesting that it is only a portion of a longer narrative. Archeologists continue to search for clues to learn more about the characters, places, and events. Some scholars suggest that this is only a summary of a much longer tale, perhaps a never-ending story.

Inspired by the Nicene Creed

I: The Orphan

"I don't have a name," the boy told him.

"You don't have a name? What do you mean you haven't a name?" the man cloaked in a tattered robe replied, his face almost entirely covered by the hood that was hanging down over his eyes. Only his chin was exposed.

"My number is three-one-six," the boy whispered. "That's what they call me."

He was afraid the guards would hear him. But he was even more afraid of the stranger who appeared in his window. Three-One-Six was one of hundreds of orphans on the Isle of Nye. The stone building filled with a labyrinth of corridors and barred windows was the only home he had ever known. He normally shared a room with three other boys but he recently had fallen ill and was quarantined in a small cell on the west wing of the compound overlooking the Sea of Midgard.

This was where many of his friends had been taken when they were sick. None of them ever came back. Only rumors of what happed to them survived. Some said the giant eel had carried them away. Some blamed the dragon. But most believed in neither the eel nor the dragon.

The stories of these beasts were older than any of the children who shared them. It was the elder children who passed down the tales to the younger. The guards would laugh any time they overheard them discussing such things. "Myths, silly myths!" they would say. Sometimes children would even be punished if they were known to make too big of a deal about the stories.

They were mostly talked about in soft voices late at night after the guards had turned in for the evening. The children would squeeze their faces through the iron bars on the windows and imagine what it would be like if the creatures were real. Using their imagination was one of the few things they could do to break the monotony of life on the Isle of Nye.

From the tales they had heard about the eel, whose name was Leviathan, they assumed he was the protector of the people. He allegedly lived in the Sea of Midgard and kept the dragon away, which was suspected to steal children. Though the details about Leviathan varied depending on the one telling the story, he was supposedly longer than the entire island and had sharp ivory fangs to fight the dragon. Their flag even had an image of a sea creature on it, though the adults said this had nothing to do with the myths.

The dragon's name was Shiloh. The only thing known of him, in addition to his name, was that he came from above the smog, which covered the entire Isle of Nye and whole of the Sea of Midgard. Most believed that the dark cloud overhead was the edge of the world and that nothing existed above it. Because the winged dragon was said to have come from above, this could only mean he was from some other world.

And the children interpreted that as meaning the dragon was evil. If he were good and powerful, the children were convinced he would fly down and try to help them, to make life better for them on Nye. And since he didn't, they figured he was either evil or that he didn't exist. It was the eel, who came from below, from their world, that they believed was the one that at least kept them safe in their compound. But these were just stories they shared to pass the time.

No one living had actually ever seen Leviathan or Shiloh. That's why Three-One-Six was certain that the man who now stood on the ledge outside of his window must be responsible for taking children who were ill. Three-One-Six was certain this was the end.

II: The Prophet

"I need you to come with me," the man told him.

"Who are you?" Three-One-Six asked in a faint voice.

"I am the prophet. I have come to set you free."

"But can you make me well?" Three-One-Six asked.

The robed man said nothing. His face was hidden in the shadow of his hood. Three-One-Six couldn't tell if he had made him angry.

"Can you make me well?" the boy finally asked again.

"Not without first making you free," the prophet answered as he pulled the hood from over his eyes revealing his face.

Three-One-Six was not sure how the man planned to get him out of the quarantine cell. And he wasn't sure he wanted him to get him out. Though I have described this as a cell, Three-One-Six never considered himself to be a prisoner. In his mind he was already free.

"We must leave at once," the man said.

"I cannot leave. I am not well." Three-One-Six said with a cough.

"We haven't much time," the man replied.

Three-One-Six started coughing louder and louder. His heart was racing. He sat up hoping to clear his chest and relieve his cough but nothing helped.

"Son, this is our moment, if you are going to come with me we must leave at once!"

Three-One-Six had never heard that word before. *Son*. What might that mean? He knew at once that he liked it. He liked it quite well. It was almost like a melody. The corners of his mouth curled upwards as he replayed the word in his mind. But his illness began to overtake him. He slumped back in his cell, the only muscles that seemed to be responding were those in his face that enabled him to form a small smile.

"Take my hand, son." The man said with urgency as he reached into the cell.

Three-One-Six's eyes were closing. He was so very weak. But when the man's hand met his he felt a spark of energy flash through his body. The man pulled him forwards allowing him to sit up.

"We must go."

"Why? Where must we go? How we will go?" the boy said.

"The eel is on his way. We cannot stay any longer."

"The eel? He isn't real." Three-One-Six replied.

"He is real indeed. And we must be moving if we are to leave."

The prophet reached his left arm into the cell and took the boy's other hand. He leaned back with his feet on the ledge pulling Three-One-Six ever closer to the bars. The boy moved through the bars as if they weren't even there. They seemed to instantly disappear before him and then reappear behind him once he was through. He felt that he would surely slip into the sea and fall to his death. But as he came through the window the man turned around and pulled him onto his back.

Three-One-Six held on with all of the strength he had, which was very little, his arms clutching the neck of the prophet. But within a matter of seconds he could no longer reach all the way around. The man was growing, and not just growing but transforming. He could hear the fabric of the prophet's robe stretching and ripping. The man's neck was now very wide and covered in large red scales.

Then Three-One-Six realized they were flying above the Sea of Midgard, only inches above the waves. The seawater splashed over them both. The cold salty water shocked Three-One-Six into being more alert. He was hanging on as best as he could as they picked up speed.

If it weren't for the water splashing him he might think he was dreaming. But this was stranger than the strangest of his dreams. He sat up slightly, leaning forward clutching onto the red scales. He turned his head backward and looked down. Towards the water he could see the silhouette of the transformed prophet. He had become a dragon.

Fear came over the boy. According to the stories, it was the dragon that stole the children. It was the eel that protected them. Three-One-Six realized he might be in great danger.

"Who are you?" the boy shouted.

Over the sound of the wind whipping past them and the waves crashing around them the dragon's response was still loud and clear. "I am Shiloh," the dragon bellowed above the roar of the water.

Three-One-Six buried his face into the back of the dragon. He clutched the sides of his neck and contemplated what he might do. He considered jumping off his back and diving into the sea below to escape. But he didn't know how to swim and he feared he would drown.

III: The Priestly Dragon

Three-One-Six finally spoke. "Where are you taking me?" he asked.

"To the mountain," the dragon said.

"What mountain?"

"Sinai," the dragon said with a thunderous voice that almost seemed to shake the sea itself.

Many moments passed without any words.

"What is Sinai?" the boy asked.

"It is the Mountain of God," the dragon answered.

"Are you going to kill me there?" the boy asked trembling.

"No," the dragon thundered. "I'm going to free you."

"But I have heard that you steal children. They say the eel is the protector of the people."

"You have heard wrong. Many years ago the eel whispered these lies to the guards and they have persisted until even this day," the dragon said.

"But the guards told me you and the eel are a myth," Three-One-Six said.

"Yes, that lie seems to be more believable to children today. You've probably heard that there is nothing above the smog too, I bet." The dragon replied.

Three-One-Six didn't respond.

The water below them began to ripple and bubble as something started to breach the surface. The dragon moved upwards but the smog sat low over the face of the sea and he seemed to respect its border. But the truth was that Shiloh could have easily broken through the smog with little effort.

"What is that?" the boy asked.

"Beware. This is Leviathan. He means us harm. Hold on." he replied.

The dragon turned quickly to the right veering out of the way as the eel came crashing into the air with fangs exposed. Three-One-Six nearly fell off, but the dragon balanced out to keep him from slipping. The boy looked over his left shoulder to see the eel as he plunged back into the sea. Three-One-Six noticed that the dragon had been wounded.

Leviathan had pierced his left wing with his fangs. Blood streamed from the bite wound.

"Are you okay Shiloh?" Three-One-Six asked.

"Hold on, my son. He will be back. We're close to Sinai now. He will not let us cross without a fight." the dragon said with a calm but serious voice.

After he spoke the dragon veered quickly to the left this time as the eel reemerged shooting into the air. But they both toppled back to the right as the eel latched onto Shiloh's right wing piercing it through with its long fangs.

Three-One-Six fell off Shiloh's back but the dragon caught him with his left wing. Shiloh slapped the eel away and wrapped his right wing around Three-One-Six. With both wings clutching the child, they tumbled down towards the water flipping end over end until the dragon regained flight. They emerged from the waves, Three-One-Six now cradled in the forearms of Shiloh. The boy was covered in blood from the dragon's wings.

"There it is son," the dragon said with a weak voice.

They could see the mountain ahead. The smog lifted upwards on the horizon. The summit of the mountain was hidden in the clouds.

"Prepare yourself. The time has come," the dragon said.

Shiloh held tightly to the boy. He first dove into the water washing the blood off of Three-One-Six in the sea then lunged forward hurling the boy towards the mountain. As they nearly reached the shore the eel broke through the waves once more and caught the dragon by his tail piercing through his flesh with his razor sharp teeth.

Three-One-Six landed on the shoreline and rolled to a stop. He immediately looked back towards the sea. The eel, having seized the tale of the dragon, plummeted back into the depths dragging him under. Three-One-Six watched Shiloh fight to resist the serpent and then finally submerge beneath the waves.

IV: The King

Three-One-Six sat on the beach waiting to see if the dragon would escape. After several minutes he began to weep. In his exhaustion and his depression he slumped over onto the rocky sand and fell asleep. His dreams were wild.

He saw the eel and the dragon fighting in the depths of the sea for quite some time. The wounds the dragon received were fatal. Finally, deep beneath the surface of the water, the dragon died.

The eel made a treacherous sound that reverberated throughout the water and echoed across the land. The eel circled around the dragon three times to his signify his victory. And then he turned towards the shore and swam forward in the direction of Three-One-Six.

In his dream he saw the eel swimming at a blinding speed. But his dream was interrupted when he heard a voice. "Arise my son," the voice said. Three-One-Six opened his eyes and began sitting up. He could see the outline of a very large, muscular man standing in front of him facing the sea.

He held a double-edged sword in both hands raised above his head. He wore a long flowing white robe with a banner draped over his shoulder. There were words written across the banner, but since Three-One-Six never learned to read he didn't understand what it said.

The boy stayed low to the ground and began to crawl backwards away from the sea. There was a great disturbance on the waters. The wind was howling. The smog had turned from gray to black and was churning in the sky. In the distance Three-One-Six could see the eel as he broke the surface of the sea moving quickly in their direction. The man stood still with sword raised high.

The eel erupted from the water charging through the air towards the man and the boy. Lightning flashed behind him between the water and the smog illuminating the silhouette of the eel as he came over the head of the man as he streched out towards the boy.

But the eel fell quickly and powerfully to the beach when the man plunged his sword into the underside of its head.

The man wielded the sword still buried in the eel lifting it from the ground and whipping it around and around and until finally hurling it out to sea. The waters turned around him creating a giant whirlpool of waves spinning and crashing.

The black smog overhead mimicked the water turning about until forming a tornado that was pulled into the whirlpool. The eel let out a screech as he sank beneath the waves. Both the eel and the smog were sucked into the abyss.

And then a light shined so brightly it initially blinded Three-One-Six. He buried his face in his hands to cover his eyes. For the first time in his life, for the first time in a very, very long time in their land, the sun was shining.

Long before, when Midgard was created, the smog had settled over the sea when the eel entered the waters for the first time. From that time on no one has seen the sun. But now both the eel and the smog had been banished. And the sun was shining brightly. A warm breeze blew across the sea. The waters turned still as it reflected the sunshine. And a melody could be heard, faint at first, then growing louder and sweeter. It was coming from the top of the mountain behind the boy.

"My son," the man said.

Three-One-Six turned around to see the man, who yielded the sword, bent down on one knee with his arms stretched out wide. The boy ran into his arms and hugged his neck. He recognized his face. It was the prophet. But his voice sounded more like the dragon. And he was wearing a crown.

"It is I, my son," the man said. "I am he who rescued you from the compound. I am he who flew you to the mountain. I am he who defeated the sea creature. I am the king of the mountain."

"Are you Shiloh?" the boy asked still clinging to the man.

"I am," he answered.

The man stood and reached down to hold the boy's hand. Three-One-Six looked down to see that he, like the man, was now clothed in a bright white robe. He took the man's hand and they began to walk up the beach.

"Alexander the Beloved," the man said.

"What is that?" Three-One-Six asked.

"It's your name," he answered as he looked down at him with a smile. "You are now my son, and Alexander will forever be your name."

The boy smiled. He had never had a name before. As they walked hand in hand towards the mountain he could begin to make out the words to the song. And more importantly he could see who was singing it. In the distance there was a multitude of children, clothed in white, singing. He recognized many of the faces. They were his friends from the Isle of Nye.

"Worthy, worthy, worthy," they sang. "Worthy is he who freed us. Worthy is he who carried us. Worthy is he who crushed the head of our enemy. Worthy, worthy, worthy, worthy is he."

AFTERWORD

I started making these dragon books for my
children four years ago to commemorate a
tale we had created about a dragon named
James who lives in the drain in the "Josephus
Bowl" at Southern Seminary. Each year I
make a new dragon story, each inspired by
a different statement of orthodoxy, that we
read on Christmas Day.

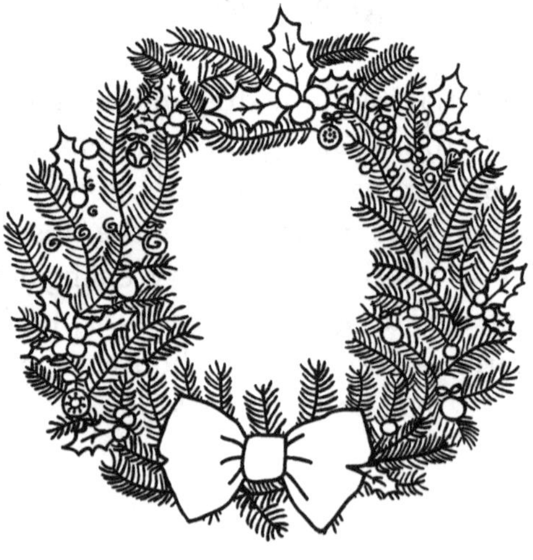

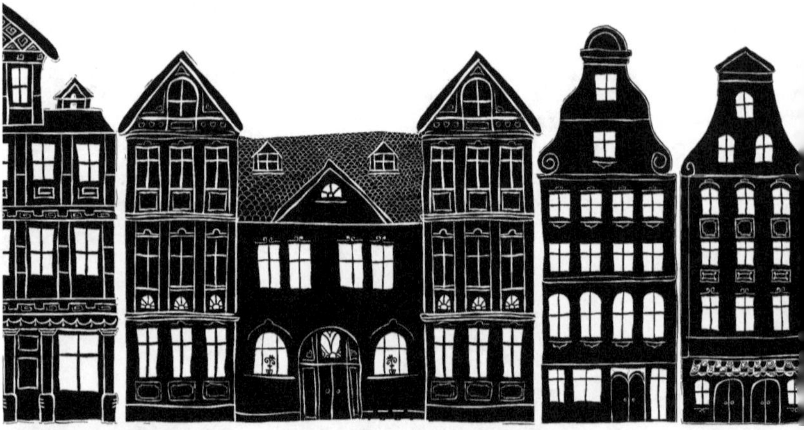

MERRY CHRISTMAS

from the

DeWitt

family

Persequendum est